SPACE DREAMS

SCI-FI Adult Coloring Book Adventure

LIGHTBURST
MEDIA

SHOW US YOUR WORK!

Send us your completed work and we will proudly share it on our feeds!

You can also email us your feedback, suggestions, compliments, comments, completed work, etc.

We love to hear from you.

t @lightburstmedia

f www.facebook.com/lightburstmedia

lightburstmedia

#lightburstmediacoloring

FEEDBACK@LIGHTBURSTMEDIA.COM

Hi.

We are glad you have decided to embark on a coloring adventure with Space Dreams.

It is recommended that you use colored pencils to color the images. If you use another medium, such as markers or gel pens, you can place a blank sheet underneath the page you are coloring. There are extra sheets of paper in the back of the book for this purpose.

We invite you to join our mailing list at lightburstmedia.com. When you join, we will send you two **bonus** coloring pages from Space Dreams. In addition, you will be the first to receive updates and free coloring pages from our upcoming books.

We sincerely hope that Space Dreams provides you with many hours of enjoyment, relaxation and fun!

Color Your Dreams,
Bonnie Bright
LightBurst Media

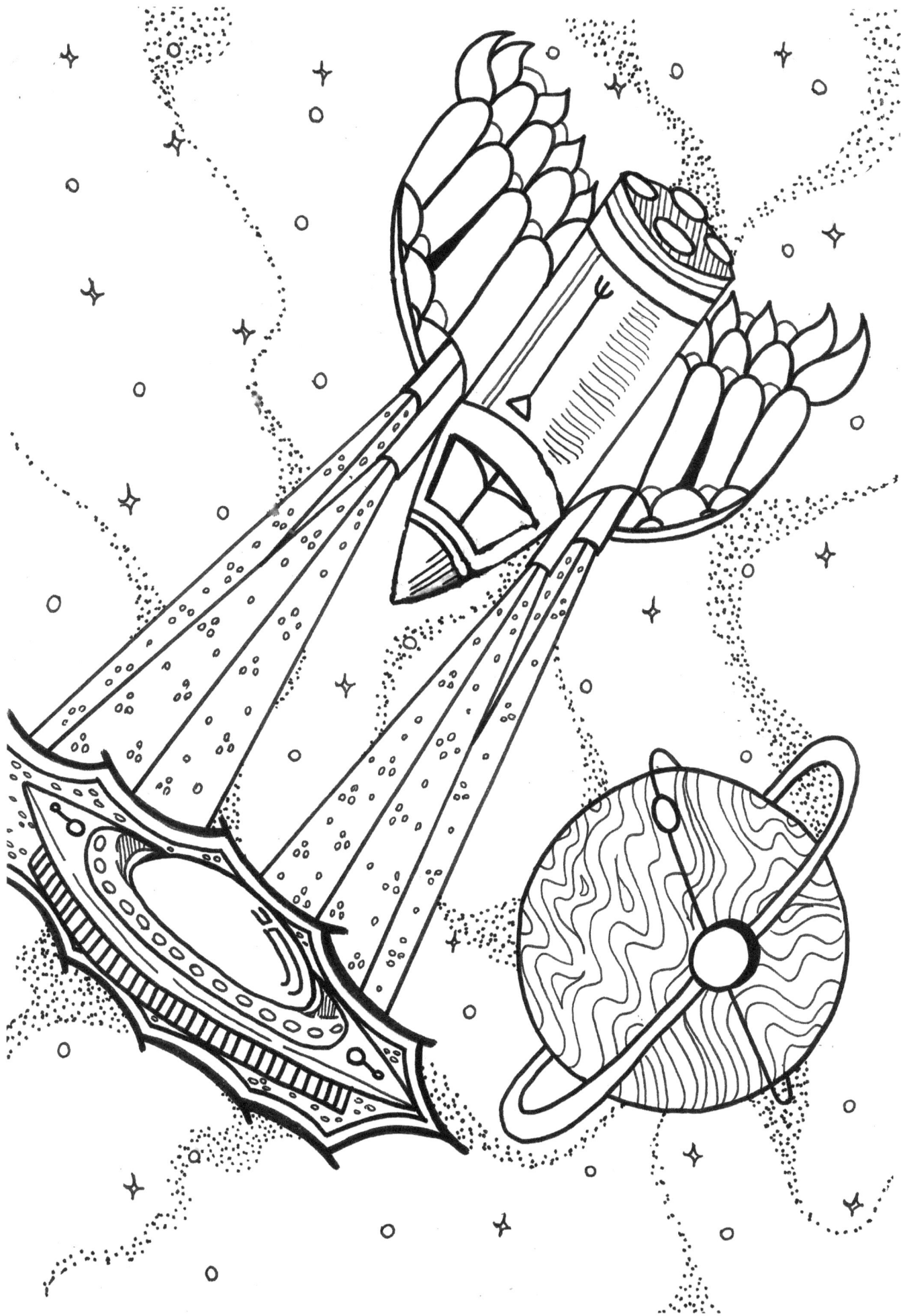

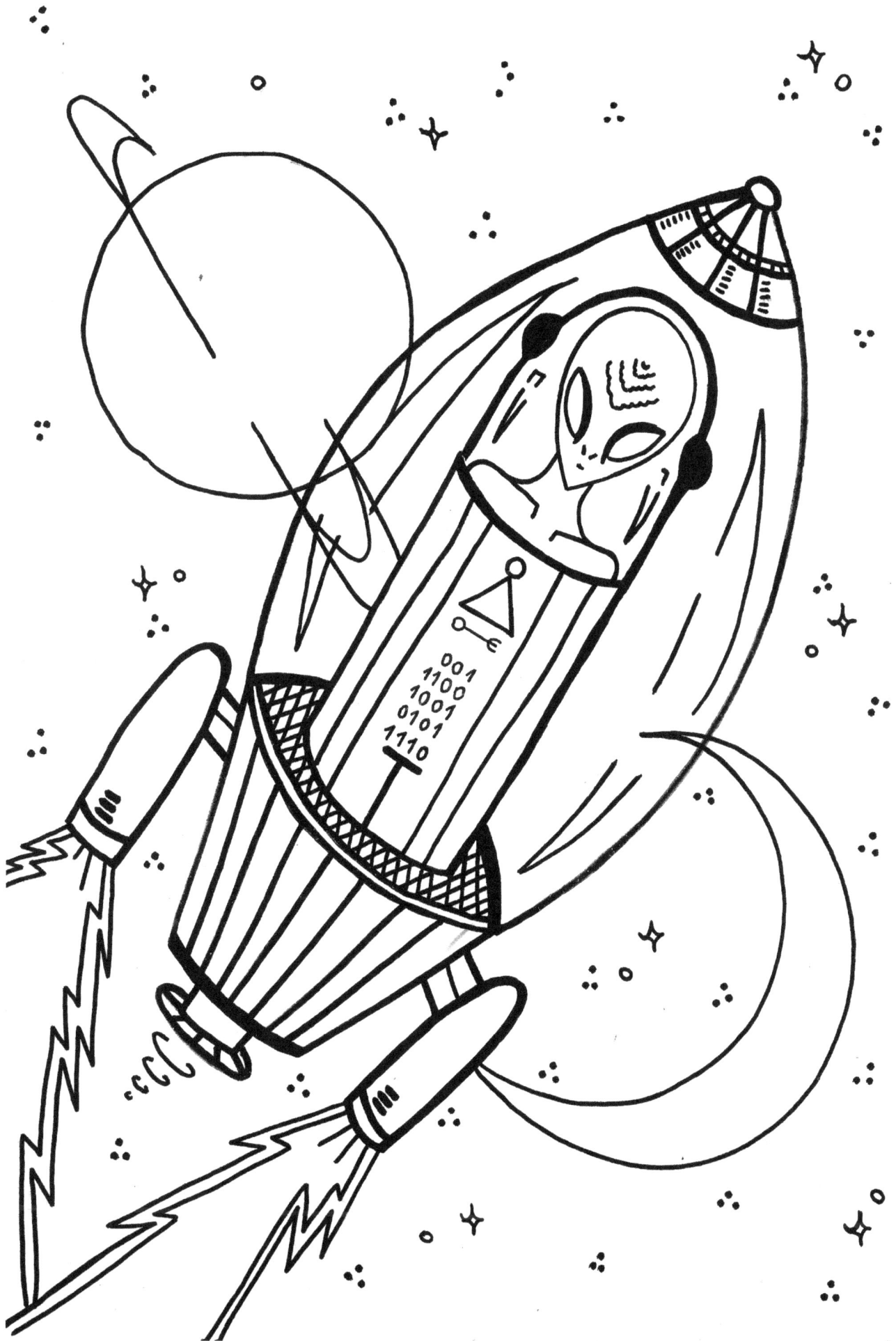

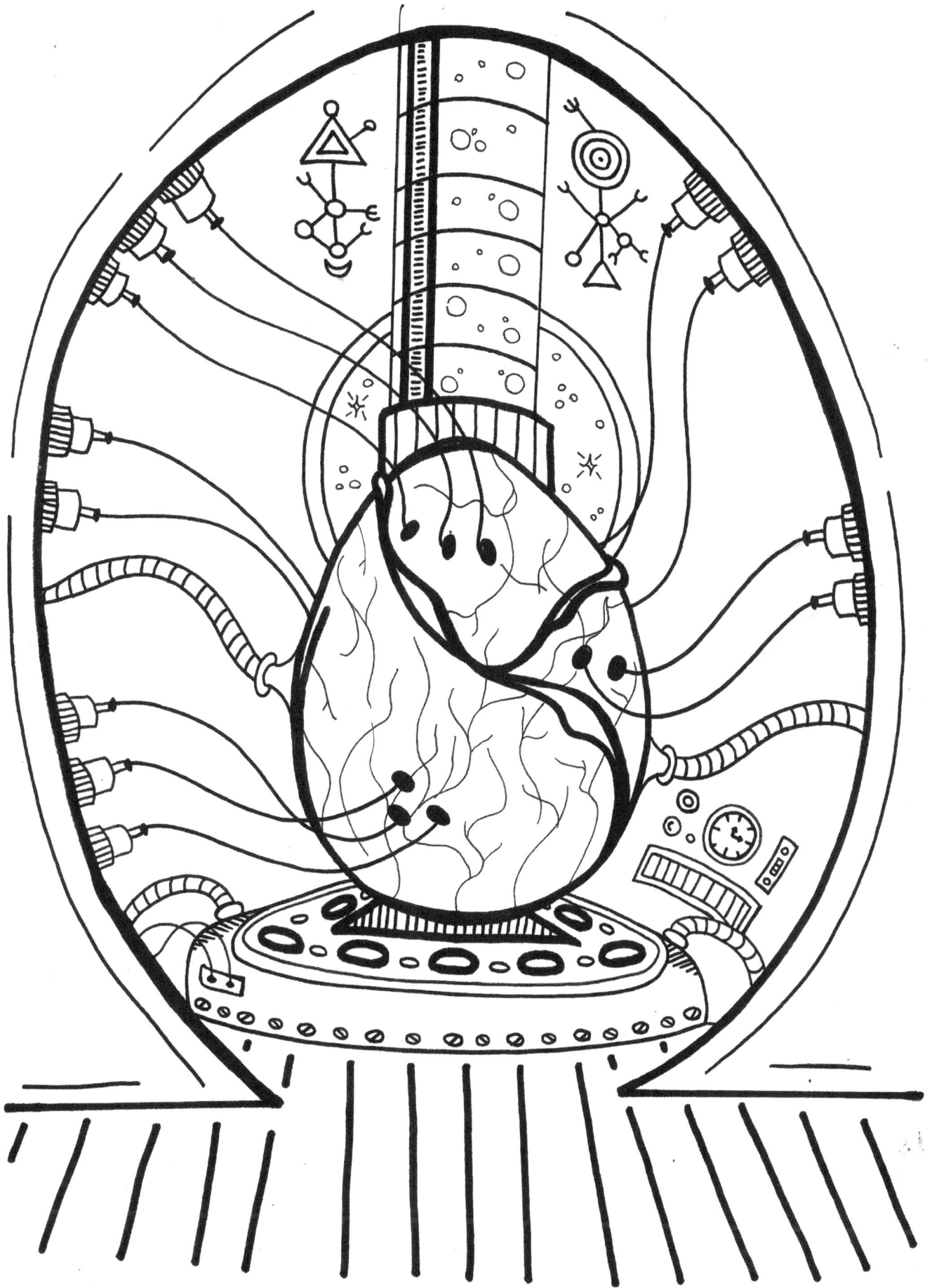

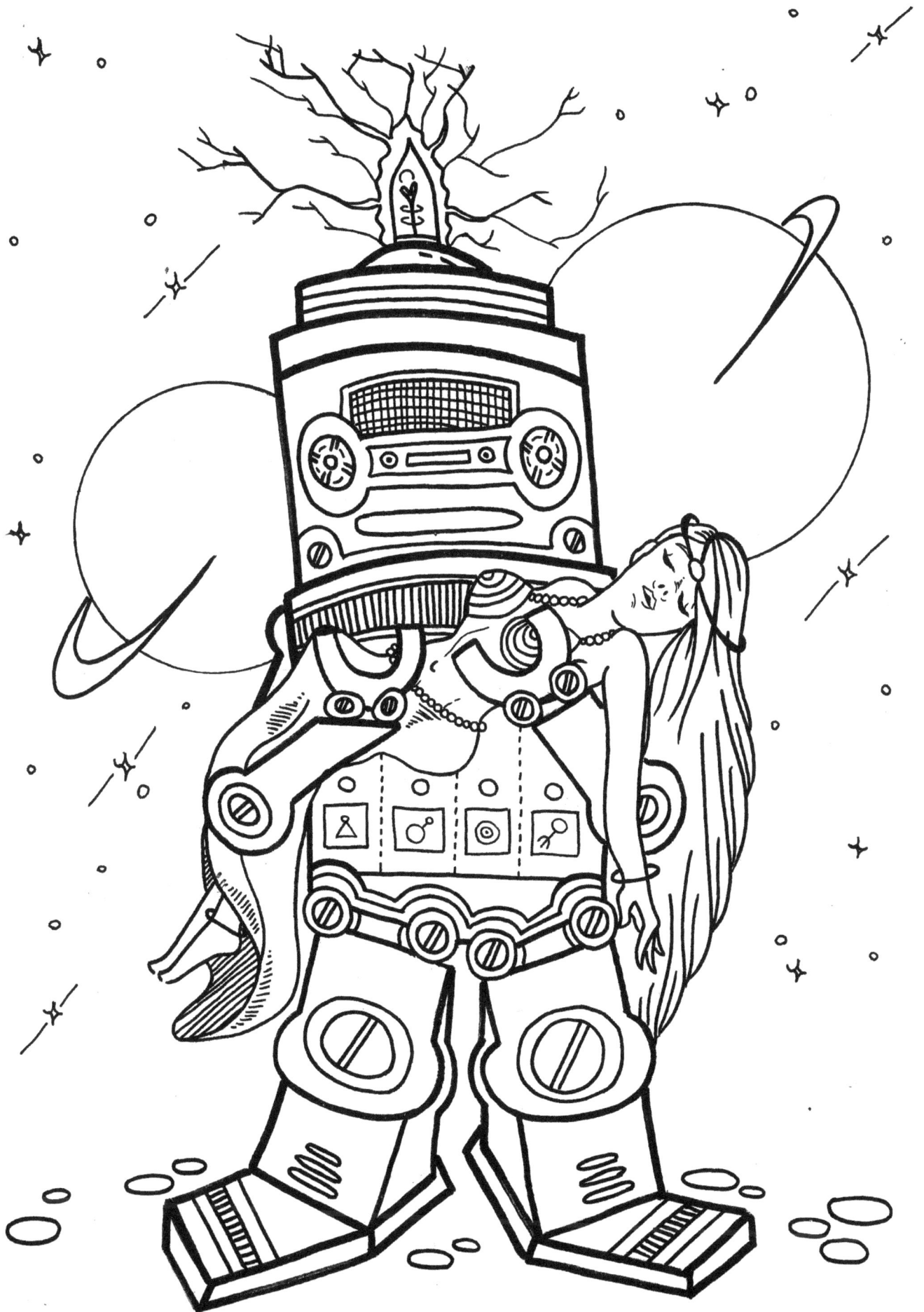

www.ingramcontent.com/pod-product-compliance
Lightning Source LLC
Chambersburg PA
CBHW081701270326
41933CB00017B/3231